The Tigris and Euphrates Rivers

The Tigris and Euphrates Rivers

By I

OCT 0 2

Watts LIBRARY

Franklin Watts
A Division of Grolier Publishing
New York • London • Hong Kong • Sydney
Danbury, Connecticut

For Ben and Thomas,
with love and thanks for your patience

Note to readers: Definitions for words in **bold** can be found in the Glossary at the back of this book.

Photographs ©: AKG London: 29; Archive Photos: 37 (Imapress); Bridgeman Art Library International Ltd., London/New York: 23 (AMQ 113701/Table from Jamdat Nasr in Iraq, listing quantities of various commodities in archaic Sumerian (early cuneiform script) c. 3200-3000 BC/Ashmolean Museum, Oxford, UK.), 19 (STC 90273/Lekegian, G. Shadufs in Upper Egypt (sepia photo)/Stapleton Collection, UK.); Corbis-Bettmann: 25 (David Lees), 34 (UPI), 5 bottom, 11, 12, 40, 52, 53 (Nik Wheeler); E.T. Archive: 28 (Louvre, Paris), 26, 27, 30 (British Museum); Gamma-Liaison, Inc.: 46 (Vioujard Christian), 43 (Chip Hires), 13 (Scott Peterson), 44, 45 (U.S. Mission/United Nations); National Geographic Image Collection: 9, 32 (Lynn Abercrombien), 8 (Otis Imboden); Panos Pictures: 38 (Chris Johnson), 48 (Daniel O'Leary), 5 top (Chris Stowers); Superstock, Inc.: cover, 2, 14, 24, 35, 42, 51; Sygma: 49 (Reza); The Oriental Institute of the University of Chicago 17; Viesti Collection, Inc.: 10 (J. Baptiste/Ask Images); Woodfin Camp & Associates: 20 (Barry Iverson).

Map by Bob Italiano.

Visit Franklin Watts on the Internet at:
http://publishing.grolier.com

Library of Congress Cataloging-in-Publication Data

Whitcraft, Melissa
    The Tigris and Euphrates rivers / by Melissa Whitcraft.
       p.   cm.— (Watts library)
    Includes bibliographical references and index.
    Summary: Traces the historic origins of how ancient civilizations developed around the Tigris and Euphrates Rivers and how modern-day civilization is affected by the two rivers.
    ISBN 0-531-11741-3 (lib. bdg.)   0-531-16432-2 (pbk.)
    1. Tigris River Valley—Civilization—Juvenile literature. 2. Euphrates River Valley—Civilization I. Title. II. Series.
DS57.W43 1999
935—dc21
                                                                               99-24120
                                                                                CIP

Contents

Chapter One
The Tigris and Euphrates Rivers 7

Chapter Two
The Beginning of Civilization 15

Chapter Three
The Ancient Civilizations 21

Chapter Four
The Wars 33

Chapter Five
The Marsh Arabs 41

Chapter Six
The Dams 47

54 **Glossary**

56 **To Find Out More**

59 **A Note on Sources**

61 **Index**

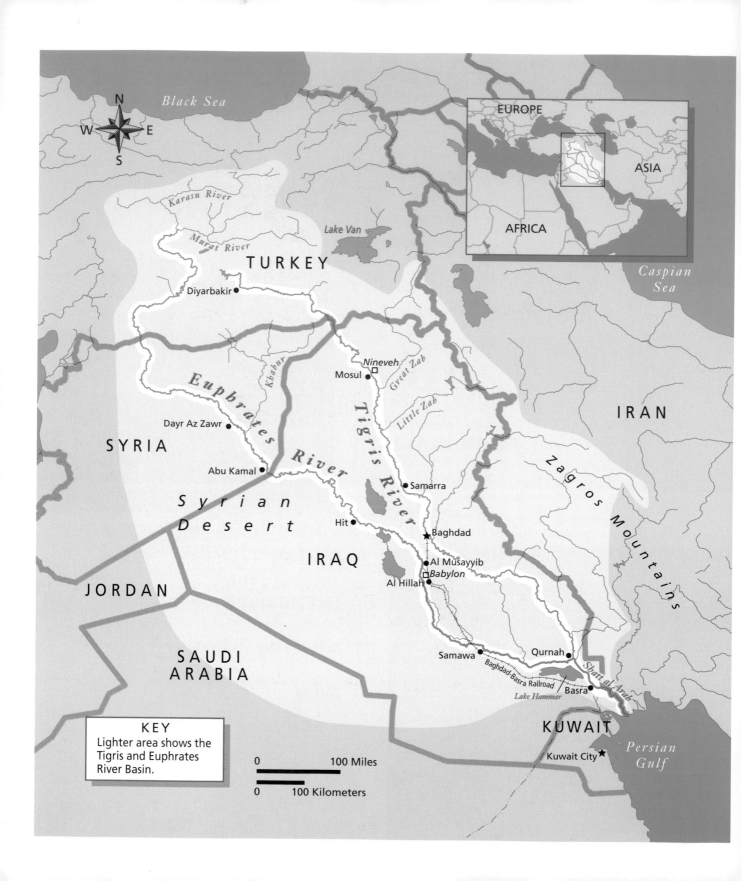

Black Sea

Karasu River

Murat River

Lake Van

TURKEY

Diyarbakir •

EUROPE

ASIA

AFRICA

Caspian
Sea

Nineveh

Mosul •

Great Zab

Euphrates

Khabur

Little Zab

IRAN

Dayr Az Zawr •

River

SYRIA

Tigris River

Abu Kamal •

Zagros Mountains

*Syrian
Desert*

Samarra •

Hit •

Baghdad ★

IRAQ

• Al Musayyib

JORDAN

□ *Babylon*

Al Hillah •

SAUDI
ARABIA

Samawa •

Qurnah •

Baghdad-Basra Railroad

Lake Hammar

Basra •

Shatt al Arab

KUWAIT

Kuwait City ★

*Persian
Gulf*

KEY
Lighter area shows the
Tigris and Euphrates
River Basin.

0   100 Miles

0   100 Kilometers

Chapter One

The Tigris and Euphrates Rivers

From the eastern highlands of Turkey, two rivers twist their way through rugged mountains as they begin their long, separate journeys down to the Persian Gulf. One river is the Tigris. The other is the Euphrates. Often, people think of the two rivers as one—the Tigris-Euphrates. In fact, 120 miles (193 kilometers) from the Persian Gulf, the

Mesopotamia

Mesopotamia is Greek for "between the rivers."

Tigris and Euphrates do fold into each other to become the Shatt al Arab. However, the significance of their relationship does not end there.

The two rivers flow out of Turkey, through Syria, and into Iraq. Through Iraq, the Tigris flows to the east, and the Euphrates, to the west. The plain between and around the two rivers is called Mesopotamia. For thousands of years, the Tigris and the Euphrates have watered this plain, nurturing the civilizations that lived there.

The Tigris

The Tigris flows southeast out of Lake Golcuk in the Taurus Mountains of eastern Turkey. Before it joins the Euphrates, the Tigris will travel 1,180 miles (1,900 km). Initially, it winds

Shepherds herd their sheep and goats along the Tigris River. Diyarbakir is the town in the distance.

through deep canyons and narrow mountain gorges before it passes through the ancient town of Diyarbakir. The Romans founded Diyarbakir in 230 BCE. It is now an important agricultural center.

After Diyarbakir, the Tigris passes through a barren strip of land that includes a 20-mile (32-km) stretch of the Turkish-Syrian border. The river then flows down into the dry plateau of northern Iraq and passes between the modern city of Mosul

Early morning fishermen lay their nets in front of the old port city of Mosul.

Iraq's 169,235 square miles (433,242 square km) are divided into three geographic regions: the Meso-potamian **basin**, the Tertiary Mountains, and the Syrian Desert.

and the ruins of ancient Nineveh on the opposite bank. Further south, two major **tributaries**, the Great Zab and the Little Zab, join the Tigris from the northeast.

Continuing south, the Tigris passes the city of Samarra. Around 5500 BCE, this region was part of the Samarran civiliza-tion. Today, with a population of approximately 24,746, this city is a pilgrimage center for Shi'ite Muslims. After Baghdad, the capital of Iraq which stands on its western bank, the Tigris veers east and enters the vast 10,000-square-mile (25,600 square km) **alluvial** lowland of southern Mesopotamia.

Flowing southeast once more, the Tigris joins the Euphrates River at Qurnah. Qurnah is thought to be the site of the biblical Garden of Eden, where human life began.

The Tigris passes through the modern-day city of Samarra.

When the two rivers join, the combined river is called the Shatt al Arab. This river flows 40 miles (64.4 km) down to Basra, the second largest city in Iraq and a major commercial center since the nineteenth century. The final stretch of river, which forms the border with Iran, passes through date orchards, rice paddies, and marshes before emptying into the Persian Gulf.

The Journey of the Euphrates

Like the Tigris, the Euphrates starts its journey in the jagged mountains of southern Turkey. Formed by the **confluence** of the Karasu and Murat Rivers, the Euphrates rushes through rocky gorges before it leaves Turkey and enters Syria.

The Euphrates passes through Syria for approximately 300 miles (483 km). The Syrian Desert surrounds the Euphrates as it winds east-southeast through a narrow channel. The land surrounding the river has been **irrigated** and is one of Syria's most successful agricultural regions. Along the way, the river travels through the ancient city of Thapsacus, once a Roman outpost.

Soon two tributaries, the Balikh and the Khabur, flow in from the east. After the Euphrates passes Dayr az Zawr, the

The Euphrates River begins its journey in Turkey.

On its journey through Syria, the Euphrates River passes by a Crusader castle.

river flows into a wider valley. Islands with vegetation appear. When the Euphrates crosses into Iraq at Abu Kamal, there are even more cultivated islands, and large irrigation water wheels dot the landscape.

After the town of Hit, the Euphrates bends toward Baghdad and creates the alluvial lowland it shares with the Tigris. When the Euphrates passes through Al Musayyib, it splits into two branches, the Hindiya and the Hilla.

At the town of Samawa, the river flows back into one channel. Here, the Baghdad-Basra railroad crosses the Euphrates. The famous ruins of Ur are inland and 50 miles (80.5 km) south. Perhaps the most celebrated of the area's ancient cities, Ur was the center of the world in the third **millennium** BCE.

After Samawa, the Euphrates flows through shallow Lake Hammar before it reaches the Shatt al Arab. By this time, the river has traveled 1,700 miles (2,735 km). When the river is finally linked with the Tigris, it flows out of legendary Qurnah into present-day Basra, Iraq's link to the Persian Gulf.

The Persian Gulf

The Persian Gulf, an arm of the Arabian Sea, stretches 600 miles (965 km) from the mouth of the Shatt al Arab to the Strait of Hormuz and the Gulf of Oman. Because the Persian Gulf is a vital shipping outlet for the countries that surround it, countries often battle to control it. During the Persian Gulf War in 1990 and 1991, the Gulf was heavily mined, and massive oil spills damaged its marine life. In this picture, fishing boats work along the Shatt al Arab waterway separating Iraq and Iran.

Here is what the Mesopotamian plain looks like today in Iraq.

Chapter Two

The Beginning of Civilization

Today, much of what was ancient Mesopotamia is a wasteland of burning sand and swirling dust storms. Little rain falls. In the southern plain between Baghdad and Basra, rainfall averages only 4 to 6 inches (100 to 150 millimeters) per year. In Mosul, to the north, the rate increases slightly to 12 to 16 inches (300 to 400 mm) per year. Temperatures drop sharply in the winter, but the summers are very hot. In the summer, the average temperature is around 95 degrees Fahrenheit

(35 degrees Celsius), but temperatures as high as 122° F (50° C) are not uncommon.

How can this barren, arid world be the mythical home of the lush Garden of Eden, where, in Sumerian mythology, there was no sickness or death and fresh water always flowed? How can this desert ever have been described as the "cradle of civilization"?

On a map, the Tigris and the Euphrates appear to be mirror images. The two rivers create a boundary that traps the land inside. When the rivers flooded in the spring, they spread alluvial silt from the north over the land. The silt fertilized the land with minerals and organic material. After the floods, however, the rich soil dried up again. The land needed a continuous supply of fresh water. The land needed to be irrigated. Who brought life to the dry, prehistoric world of sand and seasonal flooding?

The First People

The ancestors of the first farmers were hunter-gatherers who wandered the hills between Mesopotamia and the Zagros Mountains of present-day Iran. These **neolithic** people followed herds, lived in caves, and wore animal skins. Their evolution is one of the great developmental events in history because it shows how nomadic groups settled into permanent communities.

The first change in civilization occurred when people began to keep herds rather than follow them. Initially, people

What Is a Nomad?

A **nomad** is a person who has no permanent home and moves from place to place in search of food and shelter.

16

A Solid Link Between Hunters and Gatherers

Robert J. Braidwood, an archaeologist from the University of Chicago's Oriental Institute, discovered the link between the hunter-gatherers of the Zagros hills and the farmers of lower Mesopotamia. He excavated a site called Qalat Jarmo in northern Iraq in 1950 and found fifteen levels of settlement that spanned approximately four hundred years.

The levels closest to the surface indicated that the inhabitants had been farmers. Braidwood uncovered the remains of mud huts (some with ovens and chimneys), stone tools, seeds, and broken pots.

At the lowest levels (which were farther back in time), Braidwood found crude stone hoes and cultivated grains. He also found the small bones of domesticated sheep and goats. In addition, wild ass and gazelle bones were plentiful. The people might have farmed, but they also hunted and gathered grains as well.

kept wild sheep and goats. Soon they added wild boars, which evolved into domestic pigs; and **aurochs,** which became cattle. To control the herds, the people moved them from pasture to pasture instead of letting the animals roam over the hills.

The **domestication** of grains followed the domestication of wild animals. Nomads used the barley and wheat they found growing wild. Around 7000 BCE, people began to plant wild wheat and barley in small plots. To care for their crops and their herds, people settled in crude villages. Eventually, those early farmers migrated from the hills down into Mesopotamia, the fertile land between the rivers, where they could find water.

Archaeologists have estimated that by 5000 BCE, the people who had moved to lower Mesopotamia from the hills were using the Euphrates to water their land. Initially, they simply carried river water to the crops. In time, they began to channel the water to the fields by building small earth dams and ditches. They used the *shaduf,* a counter-weighted bucket that helped move water from the river to canals.

To keep the water flowing and the crops growing, the entire community worked together. Engineers designed and built dams and ditches. People charted the river's current through the canals that spread out into the fields.

Eventually, the people of Mesopotamia grew more food than they needed. That security gave people the freedom to develop nonagricultural skills. Some people became potters, while others learned weaving and metalworking. People divided up the labor and traded food for pots or plows for blankets.

Gradually, the society grew more complex. People built palaces and temples, traded goods for jewels and chariots, worshipped gods, and even wrote poetry. The early farmers who had settled on the Euphrates were now citizens of Sumer, one of the world's greatest civilizations, which eventually stretched from present-day Baghdad to the Persian Gulf.

This picture taken in Egypt in the nineteenth century shows a shaduf and how it works. It is based on the ancient design.

An example of cuneiform writing shows how pictures represented ideas.

Chapter Three

The Ancient Civilizations

Archaeologists once considered Babylonia and Assyria to be the oldest civilizations in Mesopotamia. Babylonia dates from approximately 2500 BCE; and Assyria, from the ninth to the seventh centuries BCE. After they uncovered Sumerian sites, however, archaeologists realized that Sumer's advanced culture was much older than that of either Assyria or Babylonia. By 4000 BCE, major trade routes connected Sumer north to the plateaus of Iran and Iraq and east

How the Wheel Was Invented

Archaeologists believe that the first wheel evolved from a potter's wheel that was turned on its side.

across all of southern Turkey. Sumerians also traded as far away as Egypt.

Archaeological discoveries have taught us much about Sumerian life. We know Sumerians invented the plow, the sickle, and the wheel. Sumerians also invented writing. Initially, they recorded their harvests and crop surpluses. Eventually, texts recorded history, poetry, legends, and religious rites. Texts also detailed construction plans and explained mathematics. Important astronomical events were documented. Plants and animals were categorized. Some texts offered medical advice. One text even discussed discipline problems between a father and his adolescent son.

A Different Kind of Sign Language

The Sumerians devised a way of expressing language in signs. At first, the signs were **pictographic** symbols, like icons, that evolved into a system of sound symbols. The signs were carved into clay tablets with a wedge-shaped writing tool called a **stylus.** This method of writing is called **cuneiform**, for *cuneius*, the **Latin** word for *wedge*. However, the cuneiform system was so complicated that only the scribes, or writers, could use it.

The First Libraries

Sumer left behind great libraries. At the ancient city of Nippur, archaeologists found more than thirty thousand tablets. Today, about 250 linguistic scholars can decode ancient Sumerian writing.

A clay cuneiform tablet from Iraq lists quantities of various goods in Sumer (c. 3200-3000 BCE).

The City of Eridu

The first major city of Sumer was Eridu, now called Abu Shahrein. The only remains of Eridu are low sand mounds and barren, sun-baked mudflats. The shifting river left the city behind. When Eridu flourished, however, the watered, marshy soil of the Euphrates surrounded it. Rice was a native crop, and irrigation techniques ensured fertile fields.

A reconstructed ziggurat at Ur shows us what the temple might have looked like.

Because they had few trees and no stones, the initial inhabitants, who dated from 5900 BCE, built their village huts out of river reeds and mud. Later, Sumerians used sun-dried bricks.

The cultural center of Eridu, as in all Sumerian cities, was the temple. Each city had its own god. Eridu's was Enki, the god of wisdom and sweet waters. Enki was often depicted with two streams, the Tigris and Euphrates, flowing from his shoulders or from a vase. Sumerians believed that Enki taught the people the art of writing.

The first temple of Enki was a simple platform built in the center of a small shrine. However, as century followed century, the simple temple evolved into a massive stepped pyramid called a **ziggurat.**

Life revolved around each city's ziggurat. A king governed the city, but priests were also very powerful. In addition to their religious duties, the priests oversaw harvests, stored crops, organized trade, and recorded the community's finances. The ziggurat was always bustling with activity.

Soon after 3500 BCE, Eridu was abandoned. It was not, however, the end of Sumer. It was only the beginning.

The City of Ur

Ur was 15 miles (24 km) east of Eridu. Thirty thousand people lived in houses, worked in shops, and traded in markets that spread out from the city's mammoth ziggurat. Dedicated to the moon god, Nanna, and his wife, Ningal, the ziggurat had a 150-to-200-foot (46-to-61-meter) base and stood 80 feet (24 m) high.

A massive irrigation system included three canals. The canals ran from Ur to the Euphrates. One canal even flowed directly into a harbor where boats loaded and unloaded goods within the city.

The river flows by a ziggurat and the ruined walls of the ancient Sumerian city of Ur in modern-day Iraq. Ur is supposed to be the birthplace of the biblical Abraham.

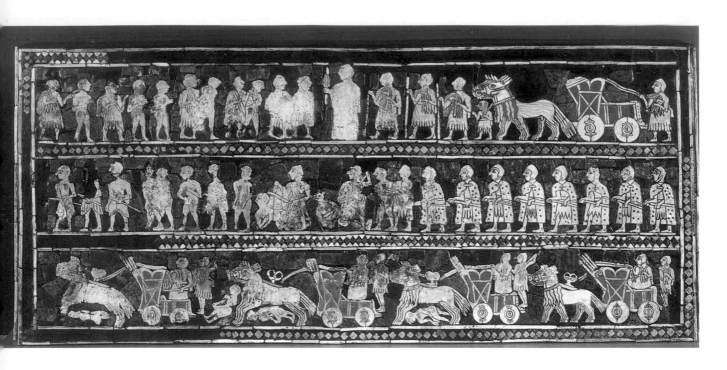

The Royal Standard of Ur shows the war side from the Sumerian Royal Graves.

Sir Charles Leonard Woolley, an English archaeologist, directed an expedition to excavate the rest of Ur between 1922 and 1934. One of his most extraordinary finds was a massive grave in which seventy-four servants had been buried along with their king. The gold instruments, ornate headdresses, and model boats made of silver confirmed Sumer's age and sophistication.

Woolley also discovered the 4,500-year-old Royal Standard of Ur. The scenes on the standard are like ancient photographs offering clues about how the Sumerians lived. On the war side, the king waits to accept prisoners. Soldiers march toward the enemy, and chariots roll over the dead. On the other side, which represents peace, the king and other royalty feast on the harvests of the land.

Sumerian culture eventually declined. The magnificent cities, with their thriving markets and glorious ziggurats, became overcrowded, and the land was less productive. Tensions grew, and cities battled cities. A people called the Akkads came out of the north in 2500 BCE and destroyed Sumer. Civilization, however, did not retreat. When the Amorites swept in from Syria, a new empire called Babylonia rose on the banks of the Euphrates.

The Royal Standard of Ur shows the peace side from the Sumerian Royal Graves (2750 BCE).

Babylonia

The greatest city of Babylonia was Babylon. Its ruins lie 56 miles (90 km) south of Baghdad. Its outer wall was 10 miles (16 km) around, 50 feet (15 m) high, and 55 feet (17 m) thick. Wide enough on top for a four-horse chariot, the wall also

The law Code of Hammurabi is written on this stone tablet.

contained huge bronze gates to control who entered and left the city.

Under the rule of Hammurabi, 2123 to 2081 BCE, Babylon thrived. Crops grew, the size of flocks increased, and trade flourished. The Babylonians worshipped Sumerian and Akkad gods along with their own. Hammurabi was most famous for his Code of Hammurabi. This document of 285 laws, engraved on a block of black basalt, combined Sumerian and Babylonian principles governing personal property, real estate, trade, business, family matters, and injuries.

Babylonians valued education. Schools taught math and legends based on gods and heroes. The *Epic of Gilgamesh* incorporated many Sumerian legends.

After Hammurabi's death, Babylonia declined, and in 689 BCE Babylon was destroyed. In 604 BCE, however, another Babylonian king, Nebuchadnezzar II, rebuilt the famous city.

The Epic of Gilgamesh

Some legends in the *Epic of Gilgamesh* predated stories found in the Bible. In one legend, a wise man called Utnapishtim told Gilgamesh a story about building a boat as a refuge from a great flood sent to punish humankind. Like Noah, the hero of Utnapishtim's story sheltered animals and his family on the boat. Because seasonal floods often swept over the Mesopotamian lowland, the inclusion of flood stories in the mythology made sense.

Famed for his leadership, Nebuchadnezzar was credited by legend for building the Hanging Gardens of Babylon for his wife. Living in the flatland of Mesopotamia, she missed the hills of her native country. Nebuchadnezzar built a brick terrace approximately 400 feet (122 m) square and 75 feet (23 m)

This picture represents what an artist thought the Hanging Gardens of Babylon might have looked like.

29

above the ground. Water pumped up from the Euphrates transformed the terrace into a lush garden filled with trees, flowers, and bushes.

Assyria

The Assyrian empire grew up along the Tigris. Its most famous city was its capital, Nineveh, near present-day Mosul. Nineveh prospered between 704 and 612 BCE. Fifteen gates,

This Assyrian bas-relief from the Palace at Nineveh (650 BCE) shows a man cultivating sugar on the riverbank.

each named for a particular Assyrian god, led into the walled city.

Extraordinary treasures have been uncovered in Nineveh. The nineteenth century archaeologist Austen Henry Layard described ". . . no less than seventy-one halls, chambers, and passages." Huge alabaster panels—documenting Assyria's wars, victories, and successes as a civilization—decorated the walls. Layard also excavated twenty-seven doorways guarded by sphinxes and huge winged bulls.

Layard's most significant discovery was the library of King Ashurbanipal, who ruled Assyria between 669 BCE and 626 BCE. Ashurbanipal had collected cuneiform tablets from all over Mesopotamia. The 24,000 tablets included scientific texts, legends, religious works, and even jokes.

Ashurbanipal's empire did not last long after his death. By 612 BCE, the Medes of northern Persia and other tribes that swept east from Arabia had destroyed most of Assyria.

For the next two thousand years, many different groups— including Persians, Greeks, Romans, Arabs, and Turks left their mark on Mesopotamia. However, no culture ever equaled the wonders of Sumer, Babylonia, and Assyria.

This sunken ship named Wisteria has been in the harbor in Basra, Iraq, since the beginning of Iraq's eight-year war with Iran.

Chapter Four

The Wars

The ancient cities of Mesopotamia now lie in ruins, but the conflicts that brought about their downfall continue. Territorial strife still dominates life between the rivers. Iraq and Iran, for example, have fought over the Shatt al Arab for centuries because this important waterway has a clear access to the Persian Gulf.

War with Iran

The most recent conflicts between the two countries began in the 1970s. In September 1980, Iraq's president, Saddam Hussein, attacked Iran. Heavy fighting along the Shatt al Arab soon spread,

The Ayatollah Khomeini is being greeted by followers in Iran.

and Iraqi soldiers battered Iran along an 800-mile (1,287-km) border.

Hussein thought Iraq would win the war easily. Iran, however, united behind its religious leader, Ayatollah Ruhollah Mussaui Khomeini, and the fierce war dragged on for years. There were as many as a million people who died in the war. Iraqi pilots bombed Iranian airfields and its capital, Tehran. The Iranians retaliated by bombing Basra, its important oil **refineries,** and Iraq's capital, Baghdad.

In the Middle East, religious differences often intensify political differences. For example, hostilities exist between the Jewish state of Israel and its Islamic neighbors. Islamic countries also fight among themselves.

Ethnically, Iraqis and Iranians are both Arabs. Most of the people of Iraq and Iran are descended from the Arab people who first appeared in Mesopotamia in the ninth century. However, Iran and Iraq follow separate branches of the religion of Islam. Islam was founded in 622 BCE by the Arab prophet Muhammad. After Muhammad died in 632, members of his family formed separate branches of Islam.

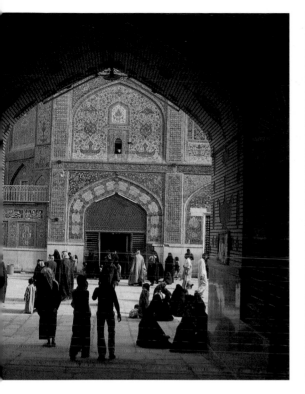

In the Middle East today, the two most important Islamic sects are the Shi'ites and the Sunnis. Iran is ninety-three percent Shi'ite; however, most Iraqis are Sunnis. Although the Iraq-Iran war in the 1980s was fought over the Shatt al Arab, it was also a religious crusade. Khomeini hoped to destroy Iraq, a nation of "infidels" or nonbelievers.

In August 1988, Iran and Iraq finally accepted a cease-fire put together by the United Nations. To avoid additional conflict with Iran, Saddam Hussein decided to build a deep channel into Iraq's Gulf port, Umm al Qasr. By establishing a modern commercial transportation system at Umm al Qasr, Iraq would not have to rely so heavily on the Shatt al Arab.

Two different mosques in Iraq where Moslems worship: Left, Iman Ali Mosque; Right, Kadhimuin Mosque in Baghdad

The Gulf War

Developing the port, however, heightened hostilities between Iraq and Kuwait. Umm al Qasr is across the water from the Kuwaiti islands of Warba and Bubiyan. Hussein wanted to lease those islands from Kuwait to ensure Iraq's control of the area. Kuwait refused. The refusal made Hussein believe that Kuwait, with its strong ties to the United States, wanted to destroy Iraq economically. Iraq would be unable to compete in the international marketplace if it couldn't ship its oil and agricultural products.

On August 2, 1990, Hussein took action. The Iraqi army invaded Kuwait and claimed the country as its nineteenth province. Outraged, the United Nations gave Iraq until January 1991 to withdraw from Kuwait. An international coalition led by the United States threatened force and retaliation.

Hussein refused to retreat. On January 17, 1991, coalition bombers, led by the United States, attacked strategic targets in Iraq. For the next five-and-a-half weeks, bombs fell on major

Iraqi cities, airports, missile sites, and oil refineries. On February 24, United Nations ground troops attacked.

By February 28, the Persian Gulf War was over. The coalition forces had crushed Saddam Hussein's scheme to take over Kuwait. Iraq was in shambles. Thousands of its citizens were dead or wounded. Its cities and defense structure lay in ruins.

Basra suffered even more damage in the Gulf War than it had during the Iran-Iraq war. All but two of its water treatment plants were demolished, and raw sewage poured into the Shatt al Arab. Disease spread throughout the city.

Saddam Hussein ordered the invasion of Kuwait.

Baghdad, which spreads out on either side of the Tigris and has a population of approximately 2,200,000, was also severely damaged during the Gulf War. In the 1970s, Iraq's capital had thrived. The fertile plains of the Tigris guaranteed food for the people. Hussein's government had constructed new buildings, highways, and sewer and water lines. There was also a new airport. However, after the Gulf War, Baghdad was almost shut down.

People living off the collection of garbage from the ruins

All the bridges across the Tigris were destroyed, as were many of the city's water treatment plants. Residents of Baghdad who used contaminated water from the river were exposed to cholera, typhoid, hepatitis, and polio. The lack of electricity, proper medicine, and food added to the city's post-war problems.

Iraq's recovery was hampered by international sanctions that made it difficult for the country to get supplies. However, by the mid 1990s, there were signs that both cities were returning to life. In Basra, the Shatt al Arab was cleared of sunken ships. In Baghdad, the eleven bridges across the Tigris were repaired, and telephone service was restored. Perhaps in an attempt to rally the people behind him, Hussein also decided to recreate ancient Babylon. He reconstructed Nebuchadnezzar's hanging gardens and built public recreation centers. The banners that hung from the buildings read "From Nebuchadnezzar to Saddam Hussein, Babylon Rises Again."

No one knows whether mighty Babylon will rise again in Iraq. Iraq's isolation from the outside world makes it difficult to know how the country is doing. For a time after the war, Kurds in the north and the Shi'ite rebels in the south attempted to depose Hussein; however, they were unsuccessful.

The Fate of the Kurds

The Kurds are an ancient nomadic people. Eighty percent are Sunni Muslims and the rest are Shi'ites. For years, Saddam Hussein had promised the Kurds their independence. In the confusion after the Gulf War, Kurdish rebels took over large areas in the north, including parts of Mosul. Eventually, Hussein's army drove the rebels and their families back from the Tigris and into the mountains of southern Turkey. Now, most of Iraq's Kurds live in exile in crowded refugee camps away from their native homeland.

In a Marsh Arab village,
boat traffic is a way of life.

Chapter Five

The Marsh Arabs

The Marsh Arabs may lose their way of life as a result of Saddam Hussein's control over Iraq. Also called the Ma'dan, the Marsh Arabs inhabit the vast southern wetlands that spread out and down from the Tigris and Euphrates Rivers for approximately 3,860 square miles (10,000 square km).

The 500,000 Ma'dan, who live in the marshes, are descended from the Sumerians. Their present way of life mirrors the way their ancestors lived six

The Persian Gulf

Thousands of years ago, the Persian Gulf reached much farther into Iraq than it does today. The Shatt al Arab did not exist, and the Tigris and Euphrates flowed separately into the Gulf. There were no wetlands. As the sea receded, the rivers became one, and the land separated into areas of seasonal flooding, semipermanent wetlands, and permanent marshes.

thousand years ago. The Ma'dan still pole their graceful canoes through the wide channels, floating islands, and open lagoons of the wetlands. Often called "the people of the reeds," the Ma'dan use the tall, thick rushes for fences, beds, baskets, mats, and canoe poles. They also use reeds to build their houses. Called *sarifas*, Ma'dan homes often sit on tiny individual islands. Long, dark, and narrow, with a gracefully arched roof, a reed house has fancy latticework doorways and a special outdoor platform for the family's water buffalo.

Marsh Arab houses (sarifas) are made of reeds.

Using the Water Buffalo

Water buffalo are essential to the Ma'dan. They keep the buffalo for milk and butter. Water buffalo dung is the Ma'dan's only source of fuel and is used for waterproofing. They pat the dung into plate shapes, dry the plates, stack them in cone-shaped piles, and burn them in the hearth. They use dung to patch leaks in reed roofs and walls, and to seal woven reed containers used to store grain.

Cut off from the modern world, the Ma'dan live simple but difficult lives in a harsh climate. In the winter, they endure cold rain; in the spring, violent thunderstorms; and in the summer, temperatures that reach 125 degrees F (107 degrees C). Fierce winds, particularly in the summer, whip and whistle through the reeds. Whatever the conditions, the Ma'dan have adapted their lifestyle. They grow rice and dates. They fish and weave mats. Their world is their own, but it is changing.

The End of the Wetlands

Since 1991 Iraq has diverted approximately two-thirds of the flow from the Tigris and Euphrates rivers away from the wetlands. Water from the Tigris is now channeled into tributaries whose banks have been raised to keep the water from seeping back into the marshes. Almost all Euphrates water now flows into a canal that bypasses the marshes entirely. Originally called the Third River, the 350-mile (565-km) canal has been renamed the Saddam River.

Hussein believes that draining the marshes into the Saddam River will help Iraq's water supply and ensure good harvests from its agricultural basin. Iraq is also draining the marshes and forcing the Ma'dan to flee, because they are Shi'ites whose religious association ties them to Iran. Saddam Hussein believes that the Shi'ite rebels fighting him hide in Ma'dan villages. He thinks that if the villages were not there, the rebels would not be able to create a stronghold.

For the Ma'dan, the consequences of the Saddam River project are devastating. What little water remains in the marshes is overused and not well drained. Therefore, the soil is salty and less productive. In addition, as the marshes dry up, the Ma'dan can no longer use their canoes to get produce to market. Unless they live near roads, which are few and far between, they have to walk for miles and carry their crops through hip-deep mud. The Worldwide Fund for Nature has said that the damage to the marshes at Qurnah has been so severe that they "no longer exist as an ecosystem." If Iraq continues to drain the marshes, the culture of the Ma'dan will be destroyed.

A satellite view shows the destruction of Iraq's southern marshes.

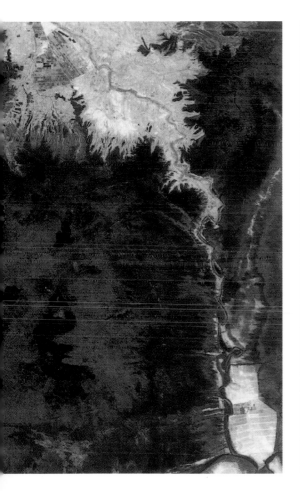

A hydraulic dam at Lake Al Assad in Syria

Chapter Six

The Dams

Historically, the success or failure of a civilization in Mesopotamia depended on its ability to irrigate the basin between the Tigris and the Euphrates. Today, however, the success or failure of modern nations depends on their ability to use the water from both rivers.

Water is precious in the Middle East. Iraq, Syria, and Turkey do not have enough water to meet the demands of their people. As their populations grow, the situation will worsen. All three countries look to the Tigris and Euphrates to solve their water shortages. However, who owns or controls the rivers?

The answers are complicated. Because the Tigris and the Euphrates both begin in Turkey, Turkey claims both rivers. Iraq and Syria, however, feel the need to protect their use of the rivers. Iraq, in particular, argues that since the Tigris and the Euphrates have irrigated Mesopotamia for thousands of years, nothing should interfere with Iraq's ancestral right to water.

Most arguments center on who has the right to control the rivers by building dams. Syria, which has the least amount of water, started damming the Euphrates in the 1960s. The Tigris flows through the country for only 30 miles (48.3 km), so a plan to harness that river has never been considered.

Harnessing the Rivers

Dams on the Euphrates allow Syria to irrigate fields and produce the wheat, barley, vegetables, cotton, and tobacco the country needs. In theory, the giant reservoirs behind the

48

dams store enough water to ensure a steady supply of water, which is vital because Syria often experiences long periods of drought.

Syria also depends on dams for hydroelectric power. The Tabaqah Dam, completed in 1973, produces thirty percent of the country's electricity. Iraq complained that the dam so reduced water flow from the Euphrates that more than three million Iraqi farmers could not irrigate their fields.

If Syria's use of the Euphrates threatens Iraq, Turkey's use of the Euphrates and the Tigris endangers both Syria and Iraq. In the 1980s, Turkey began the Southeast Anatolia Project, or GAP, for its Turkish acronym. Turkey plans to irrigate approximately 30,000 square miles (77,670 square km) of arid and semi-arid land. The country hopes to grow enough crops to feed most of the people in the Middle East. Among the 496 GAP projects are plans to build twenty-two dams and nineteen hydroelectric plants on the Euphrates by 2005.

Lack of money and international concerns about environmental consequences have kept Turkey from completing its extraordinary proposal. However, dams are being built. One of the most impressive is the Ataturk Dam, completed in 1990.

The Ataturk Dam is located in Turkey.

An Irrigation Tunnel System

Through a system of irrigation tunnels called the Sanliurfa Tunnels System, water from the Ataturk reservoir will be transported to Turkey's Southeastern Anatolian plains. Each of these tunnels is 16.4 miles (26.4 km) long and 25 feet (7.62 m) in diameter. The longest tunnels in the world built for irrigation purposes, the Sanliurfa Tunnels will distribute water to the land through a series of central and side channels. These tunnels will enable Turkey to increase crop production in the area from once a year to two or three times a year.

The Continuing Fight for Control

Turkey's actions infuriate both Iraq and Syria. The more dams Turkey builds, the more cut off Iraq and Syria are from the water they need. In fact, when the Ataturk Dam was constructed in January 1990, Turkey stopped the flow of the Euphrates for a month. Turkey insisted that Syria was warned and had time to store water. However, during that month, Syria had only twenty-five percent of the water needed to run the Al-Thawra hydroelectric plant. As a result, the plant produced only twelve percent of the electricity needed.

Turkey has no intention of curtailing its plans. When the Ataturk Dam opened, Turkish President Suleyman Demirel said that Iraq and Syria had no right to tell Turkey what to do. President Demirel reasoned that water sources in Turkey belong to Turkey the way oil found in Syria and Iraq belongs to those countries.

Regardless of Turkey's justifications, Iraq and Syria feel that if Turkey continues GAP, they will lose almost seventy percent of the water they need from the Euphrates. In addition, they worry that the water they do get, which has been released back into the river, will be contaminated with fertilizers, pesticides, and other pollutants.

To answer those concerns, Turkey has suggested channeling water from the Tigris into the Euphrates. Iraq, the only country to really use the Tigris, strongly opposes the idea. Iraq, which has four dams on the Euphrates, has three dams on the Tigris. One is in Samarra. This dam feeds water into the reservoir of Tharthar Lake through a canal 40 miles (64.4 km) long. The dam and canal protect Baghdad from flooding. Iraq also plans to set up hydroelectric plants and irrigation projects. If Turkey controls the water flow, Iraq won't be able to harness the Tigris for its own use.

The Samarra Dam in Iraq protects Baghdad from flooding.

Because it is downriver from both Turkey and Syria, Iraq has the least say over what happens upriver. One reason Iraq gave for draining the marshes was to free the country from its dependence on dam development in Syria and Turkey.

Syria and Iraq both feel that water should be released through a mathematical formula based on a country's need. Turkey thinks each country should be given the same amount of water its neighbors have, regardless of need. Syria and Iraq also support classifying the Tigris and the Euphrates as international rivers. Any projects built on the rivers would have to be coordinated with all the countries that use the rivers.

The Future

Reaching a final resolution will be difficult. Turkey resents Syria's support of the Kurdish rebels who are fighting for recognition in Turkey. Syria fears that Turkey's plans for the Euphrates will leave Syria totally dependent on Turkey for its water.

Friction also divides Syria and Iraq. Syria insulted Saddam Hussein by inviting officials from Iraq's opposition parties to its capital, Damascus, to discuss overthrowing the Iraqi president. Iraq trusts neither Syria nor Turkey because

those countries supported the United Nations during the Gulf War.

At the Baghdad Museum, on an ancient rock, is a five-thousand-year-old etching of two people shaking hands. The etching is thought to be the first depiction of the universal act of tolerance, acceptance, and peace. Perhaps people from Turkey, Syria, and Iraq will recognize the etching as a symbol of the best way to resolve the struggle over these great rivers that supported the "cradle of civilization."

Who knows what the future will hold for these two rivers?

Glossary

alluvial silt—sandy or clay-like soil deposited by rivers when they flood

aurochs—an extinct large long-horned wild ox of Europe that is the ancestor of domestic cattle

basin—a shallow depression drained by a river

confluence—the point at which two rivers join to form another river

cuneiform—composed or written in wedge-shaped characters

domesticate—to tame from the wild

irrigate—to supply with water by artificial means

Latin—the language of ancient Rome

millennium—a thousand years of time

neolithic—a period of time in the late Stone Age when humankind developed the use of tools, pottery, weaving, animal herding, and farming

nomad—a person who has no permanent home and has moved from place to place in search of food and shelter

peninsula—an area of land surrounded by water on three sides

pictograph—a picture-like symbol that represents an idea, similar to a computer icon

plateau—an elevated, but level section of land

refinery—a factory to purify raw materials such as crude oil

Richter scale—a scale that measures, in graduated steps, the strength of earthquakes

steppe—a level grass-covered plain without any forest vegetation

stylus—a wedge-shaped writing tool

tributary—a smaller river that flows into a larger one

ziggurat—a temple tower or terraced pyramid

To Find Out More

Books

Falls, C.B. *The First 3000 Years*. New York: Viking Press, 1960.

Flaherty, Thomas H. *Sumer: Cities of Eden*. Alexandria, Virginia: Time-Life Books, 1993.

Hunter, Erica, Ph.D. *First Civilizations: A Cultural Atlas for Young People*. New York: Facts on File, 1994.

Maxwell, Gavin. *People of the Reeds*. New York: Harper & Row Pyramid Books, 1957.

Simons, Geoff. *Iraq: From Sumer to Saddam*. New York: St. Martin's Press, 1994.

Organizations and Online Sites

The Arab World in the Middle East
and North Africa
http://www.arab.net
At this online resource, you'll see a listing of all the Arabic countries with their flags on the home page. After you select a specific country that you want to investigate, there are any number of selections to choose from, including history, government, culture, transport, and links to other Arabic countries. Be sure to check out the ABCs of Arabic cuisine. Not only will you find out how the unique Middle Eastern tastes evolved, but you'll also get a dictionary describing food terms and what they mean.

Grand Circle Travel, Inc.
http://www.turknet.com
This engaging travel company's site is filled with information for the tourist or student who wants to learn more about Turkish culture. Click on "Enter the World of Wonders," and you'll find descriptions of history, culture, ancient Turkish cities, villages, natural landscape, coastal developments, etc. For example, find the section about "Participating in Turkish life" to find out why Turks hug and kiss one another on both cheeks when greeting one another.

The Academy of Natural Sciences
1900 Benjamin Franklin Parkway
Philadelphia, PA 19103
http://www.acnatsci.org
Check out this site for information on wetlands. You'll find a great article by Barry Lewis entitled "Wetlands Are More Than Mere Swamps" at
http://www.acnatsci.org/erd/ea/wetlands_short.html.

The Republic of Turkey
Turkish Embassy
Washington, DC
http://www.turkey.org
This is the Turkish embassy's site. Check it out for the latest news events happening in Turkey (but be patient as some days the site is not in working order).

A Note on Sources

Researching a book on the Tigris and Euphrates Rivers is not as easy as it looks. Because the political situation in that area is unstable, it can be difficult to find reliable information on the countries and the rivers in that part of the world.

Since I couldn't find any children's reference books or modern books on the Tigris and Euphrates Rivers, the first thing I did was go to a library and look at a map. Then I pinpointed certain cities that were located on the two rivers in order to get an idea of which cities were most important and why. After these steps, I did research on the Internet and looked in current publications, such as magazines. In this way, I was able to get some information on the cities that I knew were located on the two rivers and track down facts about the rivers as well.

Of course, I read lots of books, but these books were mostly written between 1950-1960. I tried to confirm all of the information I read in these books by looking for similar facts on the Internet or in magazines to see whether there had been any changes in the past thirty years. Although I did browse through encyclopedias for information, I think it's more important to read books and to use them as your final source, and subsequently, you can use Internet sources for filler or to confirm facts.

—*Melissa Whitcraft*

Index

Numbers in *italics* indicate illustrations.

Abraham, *25*
Abu Kamal, 12
Ali Mosque, *35*
Al-Thawra hydroelectric
  plant, 50
archaeologists, *16*, 21
Ashurbanipal, 31
Assyria, 21, 30–31
Ataturk Dam, *49*, 50
aurochs, 18

Babylon, 27–28, 39
Babylonia, 21, 27–30
Baghdad, 12, 34, *35*, 37–38,
  39
Basra, 13, *32*, 34, 37, 39
boats, *40*
Braidwood, Robert J., *16*, 17
bridges, 38, 39

canals, 25, 51
Code of Hammurabi, 28, *28*

confluence, 11
Crusader castle, *12*
cuneiform, *20*, 22–23, *23*

Damascus, 52
dams, 48–49, 50, 51
Dayr az Zawr, 11
Diyarbakir, *8*, 9
dung, *43*

earthquakes, 51
Egypt, *19*
Epic of Gilgamesh, 28
Eridu, 23–25
Euphrates River, 7–8, 10, 11,
  11, 47–48, 51

farmers, 18
fishermen, *9*, 49

GAP projects, 49
Garden of Eden, 10, 16

Great Zab, 10
Gulf of Oman, 13
Gulf War, 36–39, 53

Hammurabi, 28
Hanging Gardens of
    Babylon, *29*, 29–30
herders, 16, 18
hunter-gatherers, 16, 17
Hussein, Saddam, 33–34, 35,
    36, 37, *37*, 39, 44, 52

Iman, *35*
Iran, 11, 16, 33–35
Iraq, 8, 10, *14*, *23*, 33–35,
    36–40, 47, 48, 49, 50,
    51, *52*, 53
Iraq-Iran war, 33–35
irrigation, 11, 18, *48*, 48–49,
    50

Kadhimain Mosque, *35*
Khomeini, Ayatollah, *34*
Kurds, 39, 52
Kuwait, 36, *37*

Lake Al Assad, *46*
Lake Golcuk, 8
Lake Hammar, 13
Layard, Austen, Henry, 31

Little Zab, 10
living on garbage, *38*

Ma'dan, 41–43, 44, 45
map of Tigris and Euphrates
    River Basin, *6*
Marsh Arabs, *40*, 41–43, *42*
marshes, 44–45, *45*, 52
Mesopotamia, 8, 10, *14*
metalworking, 18–19
mosques, *35*
Mosul, 9, *9*, 15, 30
Muhammad, 34
Murat Rivers, 11
Mussayyib, 12

Nebuchadnezzar II, 28, 29
Nineveh, 10, *30*, 30–31
nomads, 16

oil refineries, 34

people of the reeds, 43
Persian Gulf, 7, 11, 13, 42

Qalat Jarmo, 17
Qurnah, 10, 13

Richter scale, 51
Romans, 9, 11

Royal Standard of Ur, 26, *26*, 27

Saddam River, 44

Saddam River project, 44

Samarra, 10, *10*

Samarra Dam, *51*

Samawa, 12

sarifas, *42*, 43

shaduf, 18, *19*

Shatt al Arab, 8, 11, 13, 33, 35, 37, 39

shepherds, *8*

Shi'ites, 10, 35, 39, 44

steppes, 12

Sumer, 19, 21–22, 27

Sumerian Royal Graves, *26*, 27

Sumerians, 22, 41

Sunnis, 35, 39

Syria, 8, 10, 11, 12, *46*, 47, 48, 49, 50, 51, 52, 53

Tabaqah Dam, 49

Taurus Mountains, 8

Tertiary Mountains, 10

Third River, 44

Tigris, 7, 8–11, 47–48, 51

Turkey, 7, 8, 9, 11, *11*, *16*, 47, 48, 49, 50, 52, 53

Umm al Qasr, 35, 36

Ur, 12–13, *24*, *25*, 25–27

Utnapishtim, 28

water, 47–48, *48*

water buffalo, 43, *43*

wetlands, 42, 44

Wisteria, *32*

Woolley, Sir Charles, Leonard, 26

ziggurat, 24, *24*, 25, *25*

About the Author

Melissa Whitcraft lives in Montclair, NJ, with her husband, their two sons, and their dog. She has a Masters in Art in Theatre and, in addition to plays and poetry, has written both fiction and non-fiction for children. She has published *Tales From One Street Over*, a chapter book for early elementary-grade readers. Her biography, *Francis Scott Key*, was published as a Franklin Watts First Book. Ms. Whitcraft has also written the *Hudson River* for the Franklin Watts Library series. Whenever possible, Ms. Whitcraft travels on rivers.